Mathematics
Revision

Paul Broadbent

Good day. I'm Sir Ralph Witherbottom. I'm an accomplished inventor, a dashing discoverer and an enthusiastic entrepreneur.

Hi! I'm Isabella Witherbottom – my friends call me Izzy. I'm Sir Ralph's daughter and I like to keep him on his toes!

And they both keep me on my toes! How do you do? I'm Max, the butler, at your service.

Woof! I'm Spotless – aptly named, as you can see. I'm the family's loyal dog.

Contents

Back to Front 4
  Mental addition and subtraction

Party Planning 6
  Multiplication

Aunt Sarah's Savings 8
  Division

Revise Time 10
  Revision exercises

Decimal Decorating 12
  Place value

Frosty Figures 14
  Ordering numbers

Factor Tree Factory 16
  Number sequences

Revise Time 18
  Revision exercises

Footy Fractions 20
  Fractions

Fair Testing 22
  Fractions of quantities

Tunnel Travel 24
  Decimals and money

Revise Time 26
  Revision exercises

Chicken Run 28
   Measures

Train Times 30
   Time

Spreading Jam 32
   Handling data

Revise Time 34
   Revision exercises

Tricky Triangles 36
   2D shapes

Shopping Net 38
   3D shapes

Car Treasure Hunt 40
   Position and direction

Revise Time 42
   Revision exercises

Glossary 44

Answers 46

Back to Front

Isabella Witherbottom was trying to solve a Thinking Puzzle from her new book. The question was – 'What do the names Eve, Hannah and Bob have in common?'

After looking at them long and hard, she noticed that each name is spelt the same whether it's written backwards or forwards. "Well done," said Max, the butler, "you solved that quickly. Those names are called **palindromes**."

It reminded Max of a backwards and forwards number puzzle, so he challenged Isabella with it. "Give me any 4 **digits** from 1 to 9, and by subtracting I'll always get the same answer: 6174."

Isabella gave Max the digits 2, 1, 5, 4. Max wrote the largest number he could make with the digits and then wrote it backwards to make the smallest possible number. He then asked Isabella to subtract the smallest away from the largest.

```
  5421
 -1245
```

Isabella found this hard, so Max explained his method. "Look at '21' on the top number. Take 10 from the 20 and give it to the 1 to make 11."

5400 + 21 = 5421

5400 + 10 + 11 = 5421

Isabella took 5 away from 11 and wrote in 6. She then used the same method to complete the subtraction with the answer 4176.

```
  5421
 -1245
  ----
  4176
```

"This didn't work, you haven't made 6174." Isabella wasn't impressed.

"Be patient, one more subtraction I think," said Max, not with a great deal of confidence.

He rearranged the digits 4176 in the same way, taking the smallest number away from the largest number.

Isabella used the same method as before to find the difference between the two numbers and now she was impressed. The answer was just as Max had said: 6174.

```
  7641
 -1467
  ----
  6174
```

Later that day, Isabella gave a challenge of her own to Max. "Give me any 3 digits up to 5 and I'll always give you a palindrome for an answer."

Max gave 1, 4 and 3. Isabella wrote the largest number and the smallest number and then added them together.

Max was impressed. "565 – a palindrome!" exclaimed Max. "Ah! The mysterious magic of mathematics!"

```
   431
  +134
   ---
   565
```

Calculation codes

Write the answers and then code letter for each digit to find the secret word.

4
1
6
5
2
3
0
p
a
e
d
m
r
u

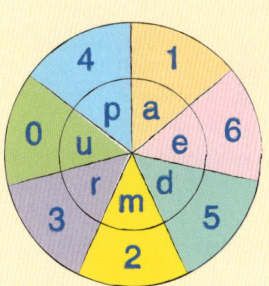

a

```
   8 1 0
 – 6 0 8
 -------
 □ □ □
```

c

```
   1 5 8 1 5
 +   5 6 9 7
 -----------
 □ □ □ □ □
```

b

```
   5 0 2 2
 –   3 5 8
 ---------
 □ □ □ □
```

d

```
   2 8 7 0 6
 +   2 8 0 7
 -----------
 □ □ □ □ □
```

Izzy and I know our maths back to front!

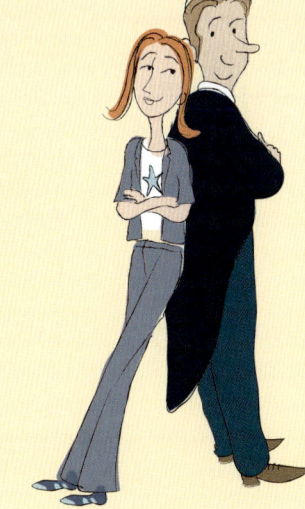

Top Tips!

If you use a column method for adding or subtracting, write the numbers carefully so they line up one above the other. Squared paper is good for lining up columns.

Did you know?

Ferdinand de Lesseps was a canal builder and designed the Panama Canal. A famous palindrome about him is:

A MAN A PLAN A CANAL PANAMA

Read it carefully backwards.

Party Planning

Max, the butler, was writing a shopping list for Isabella Witherbottom's party. He needed enough food for 24 people and wanted to work out how many packs of each item he needed.

There were 4 drink cartons in a pack. 4 × 6 = 24, so he needed 6 packs of 4 drinks. Bread rolls were sold in packs of 12. 2 × 12 = 24, so he needed 2 packs of rolls. Crisps were in packs of 8 bags. 8 × 3 = 24, so he would get 3 packs.

He then thought about the things needed for the games. Isabella wanted to have a 'strongest straw bridge' competition. Each person would be given 36 straws. Max wrote 24 × 36 in a grid to help him work out this more difficult multiplication.

×	20	4
30		
6		

Max wrote the answers in each grid space.

20 × 30 = 600	30 × 4 = 120
20 × 6 = 120	6 × 4 = 24

He added each row.

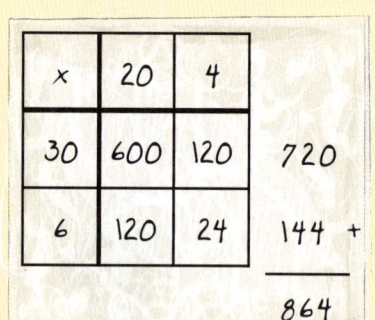

600 + 120 = 720   120 + 24 = 144

×	20	4	
30	600	120	720
6	120	24	144 +
			864

Finally he added 720 and 144. He would need 864 straws. There were 100 straws in a pack, so he would buy 9 packs and would have a few straws spare.

Birthdays definitely add on the years, even when it's not my birthday.

On the day of the party, the bridges were built and tested and the food was eaten. It was time for the guests to leave, but Max had forgotten to make party bags.

"Don't worry," said Sir Ralph Witherbottom. "We'll give away the balloons. I had 3 bags each with 10 balloons. That's 30, but 6 burst which leaves 24. Exactly the right amount!"

Colour your own card

Calculate these multiplications using the grid method. Colour the shapes with the matching answers. What is the picture on the birthday card?

18 × 23

26 × 34

50 × 17

15 × 49

22 × 35

24 × 28

Top Tips

Use small numbers to help multiply large numbers.
2 × 3 = 6
20 × 3 = 60
20 × 30 = 600

Did you know?
When you multiply a number by 9, the digits always total 9. This works even for large numbers:
3584 × 9 = 32 256 → 3 + 2 + 2 + 5 + 6 = 18 → 1 + 8 = 9

Aunt Sarah's Savings

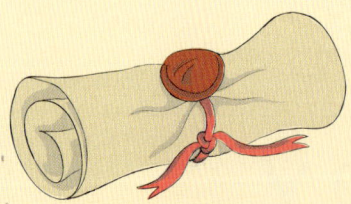

Sir Ralph Witherbottom read out a letter to Isabella and Max, the butler. "We've been left Aunt Sarah's savings in her will."

The letter explained that £800 would be given in equal amounts over 4 years. Isabella worked out how much they would get each year.

"8 divided by 4 is 2, so 800 divided by 4 is 200. That's £200 each year," she said.

The money was to be shared equally between Isabella, Sir Ralph and Max.

"We have to divide £200 by 3 now," said Max. He used a written method for this:

$$\begin{array}{r} 66\,r\,2 \\ 3\overline{)200} \\ -180 \quad \leftarrow 60\times 3 \\ \hline 20 \\ -18 \quad \leftarrow 6\times 3 \\ \hline 2 \end{array}$$

They say 'charity begins at home'. Where's my share?

"We will get £66 each year and there will be a **remainder** of £2," he continued.

"What shall we do with the £2 left over?" said Sir Ralph.

"I know," suggested Isabella, "we'll give it away to 'Dog Rescue'. That's where Aunt Sarah got her dog and they do some really good work with rescued dogs."

They all agreed that it was a good place to give the money.

Rescue remainders

Write, in words, the remainders from each division to solve the puzzle.

Across

3 214 ÷ 7
5 175 ÷ 3
7 160 ÷ 9

Down

1 140 ÷ 6
2 313 ÷ 5
4 114 ÷ 9
6 429 ÷ 10

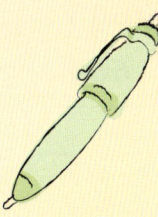

Whenever you are dividing numbers, work out an approximate answer first. You can then check this with the actual answer to see if it seems correct.

Did you know?

When you divide money with pounds and pence, you can have a decimal answer rather than a remainder:

34 ÷ 4 = 8 r 2
£34.00 ÷ 4 = £8.50

Revise Time

1 Use these numbers to answer the questions.

849   792   1235   1190   1088

a What is the total of the two odd numbers? _____
b What is the difference between the two largest numbers? _____
c Which two numbers have a total of 1880? _____
d Which two numbers have a difference of 341? _____

2 Answer these.

a   1924
  + 3568
  _____

b   2095
  + 3796
  _____

c   3928
  + 4007
  _____

d   1944
  − 1062
  _____

e   3072
  − 1993
  _____

f   2603
  − 1684
  _____

3 Write the missing digits from these.

a   3☐
  ×   9
  _____
    3 4 2

b   ☐7
  ×   4
  _____
    3 0 8

c   8☐
  ×   6
  _____
    5 0 4

d   7 2
  ×   ☐
  _____
    5 7 6

e   6☐
  ×   7
  _____
    ☐7 6

4 Complete these grid multiplications.

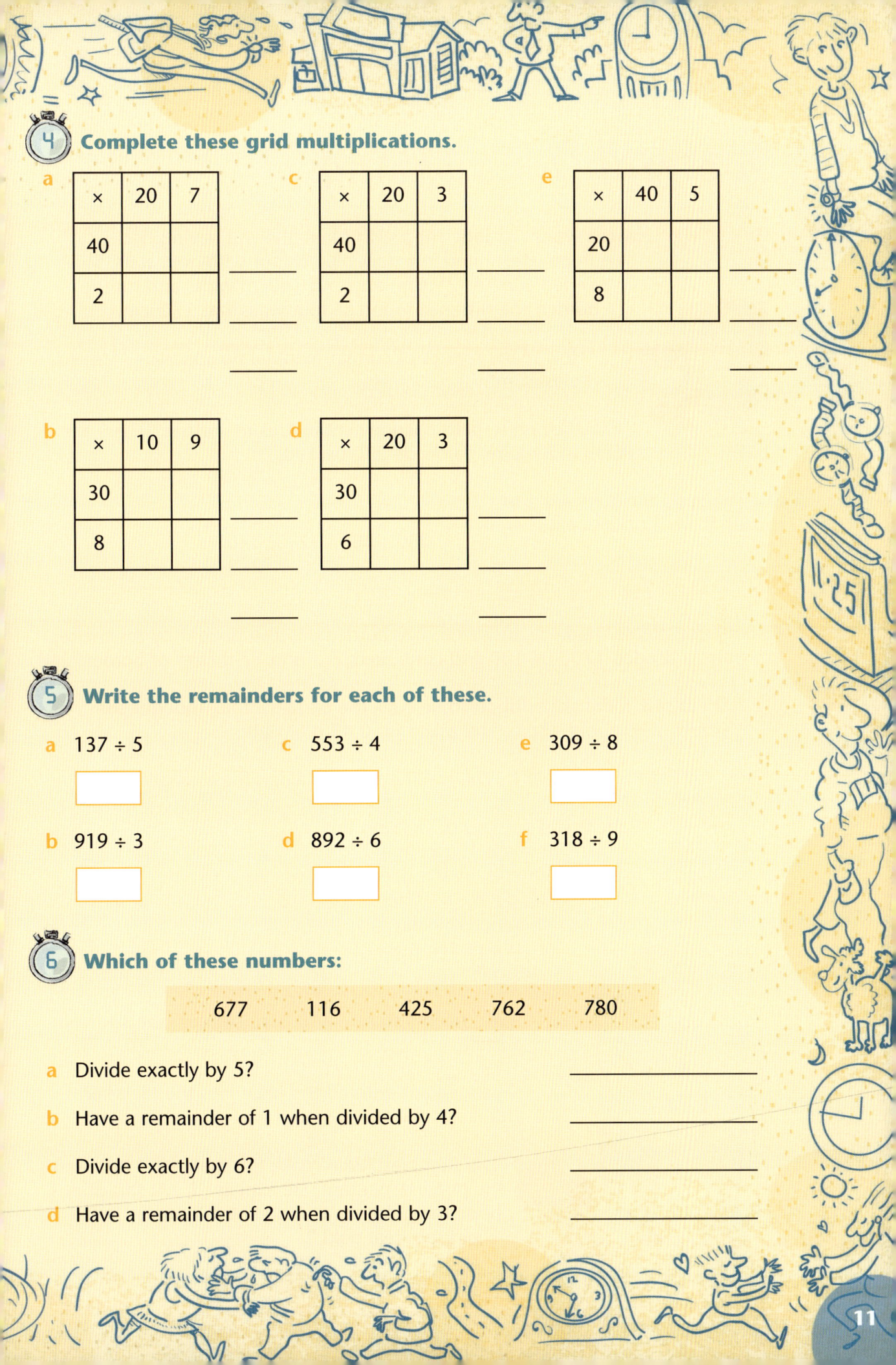

a
×	20	7
40		
2		

c
×	20	3
40		
2		

e
×	40	5
20		
8		

b
×	10	9
30		
8		

d
×	20	3
30		
6		

5 Write the remainders for each of these.

a 137 ÷ 5

b 919 ÷ 3

c 553 ÷ 4

d 892 ÷ 6

e 309 ÷ 8

f 318 ÷ 9

6 Which of these numbers:

677   116   425   762   780

a Divide exactly by 5?

b Have a remainder of 1 when divided by 4?

c Divide exactly by 6?

d Have a remainder of 2 when divided by 3?

Decimal Decorating

Isabella was in a fabric shop with Max. She was having her bedroom decorated in a dark blue colour with gold stars. She needed curtains 230cm long and 140cm wide, and for the border, the distance round all four walls was 1700cm.

"How many metres of curtain material do you want?" asked the assistant.

Max helped Isabella change centimetres to metres. "There are 100cm in a metre, so divide 230 by 100."

She imagined the numbers and moved them 2 places to the right.

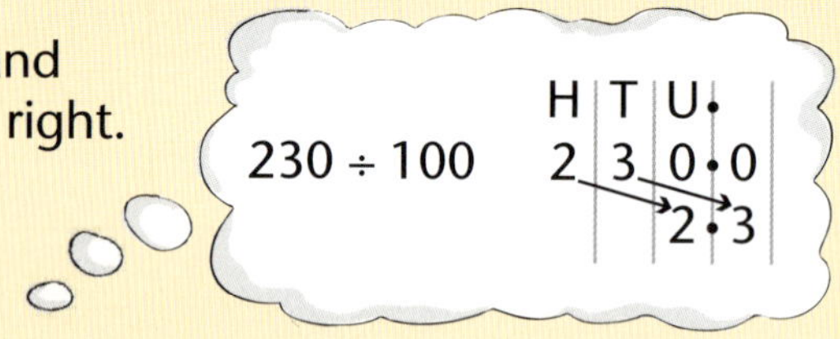

$$230 \div 100$$

	H	T	U		
	2	3	0	.	0
			2	.	3

"2.3 metres, please," Isabella answered. The border was also bought by the metre, so Isabella divided 1700 by 100 and continued, "… and 17 metres of border."

Isabella saw some gold ribbon to tie back the curtains. Max thought she would need about 48cm, and asked for 0.48m of ribbon.

"The ribbon is sold by the millimetre," explained the assistant.

Isabella was very quick working this out. There are 10mm in a centimetre, so she needed to multiply by 10. She imagined moving the numbers one place to the left.

$$48 \times 10$$

	H	T	U
		4	8
	4	8	0

At this price it's the most valuable room in the house.

"We'll need 480mm of ribbon, please," she said with a smile.

The assistant entered the price into the till. Max gaped at the **total** cost; it was very expensive.

"Did Rumplestiltskin make this material?" he asked the puzzled assistant. He explained, "At this price I hope the gold is real and I know Rumplestiltskin could spin real gold."

Decorating decimals

These boxes increase numbers by 10 or 100. Colour the ribbons each side to match the correct numbers.

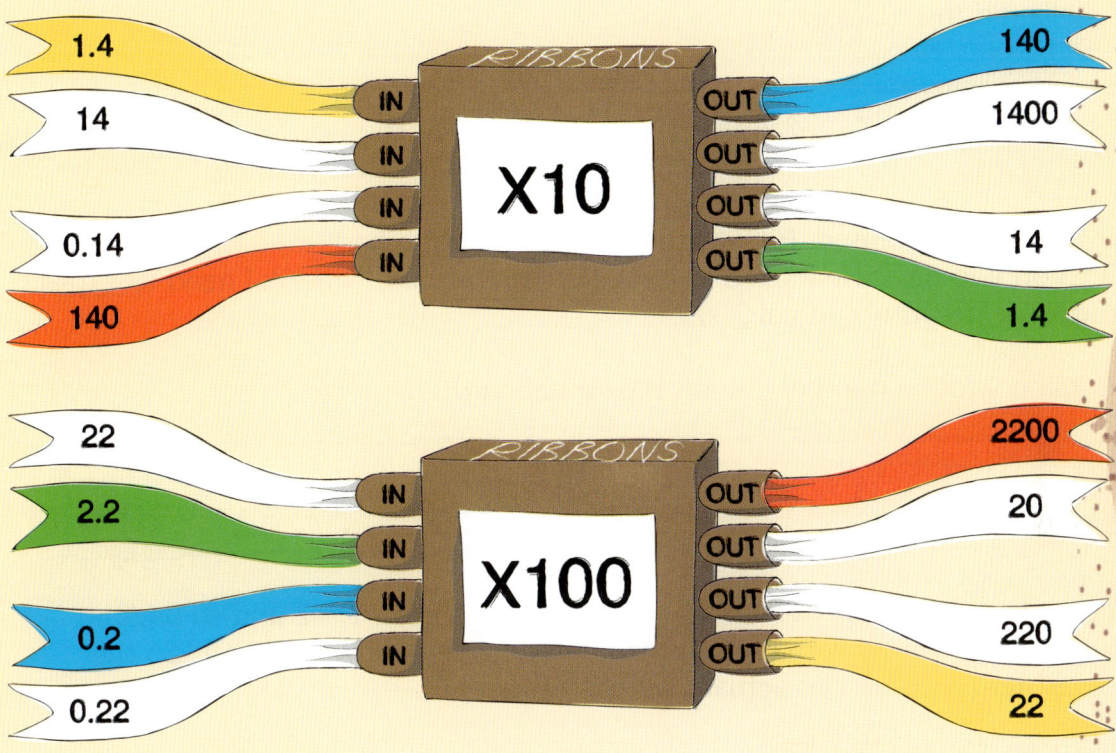

Top Tips

Zero is a very important digit when you make a number 10 or 100 times bigger. Zeros are then used to fill the spaces.
3.8 × 10 = 38
3.8 × 100 = 38**0**

Did you know?

You can set up a ×10 or ÷10 machine on your calculator. Key in the following: 10 × × 10 = and then any small number. Keep pressing the = key and watch the results.
10 ÷ ÷ 10 = and then any large number. Keep pressing the = key and watch the results.

Frosty Figures

For 20 years now, Sir Ralph had kept a record of the temperature for each day in January. Isabella asked if she could help. Sir Ralph gave her the temperatures for the last week and asked her to write them in order, starting with the highest. Isabella did this quickly:

"Finished!" she exclaimed. "The warmest was 7°C and the coldest was 0°C."

Sir Ralph was confused. He was sure the temperature had gone below freezing (0°C) on two days. He looked at Isabella's list and said, "I think I need to explain **negative numbers** to you, Izzy."

Sir Ralph wrote a number line on the whiteboard.

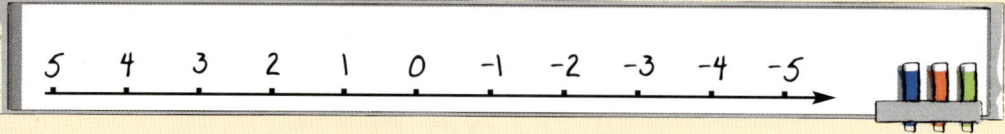

"If you keep counting backwards after zero you go to −1, −2 and so on," he explained. "1 below zero is called negative 1 or sometimes minus 1. So the coldest temperature was actually −2°C."

Sir Ralph asked Isabella to work out the **difference** between the temperatures of 4°C on Monday and −2°C on Tuesday. Isabella pointed to 4 and counted as she moved backwards along the number line to −2. The difference was 6, so the temperature had dropped 6°C.

Then he asked her to work out the difference between the temperatures on Tuesday and Wednesday. On Wednesday the temperature was 0°C. Isabella started on −2 and counted to zero. So the temperature had increased by 2°C.

This old house is so cold, even when I turn the heating up.

"Wednesday might have been slightly warmer than Tuesday, but still a bit too close to zero for my liking!" shivered Isabella.

Temperature test

Write the missing numbers on each thermometer.

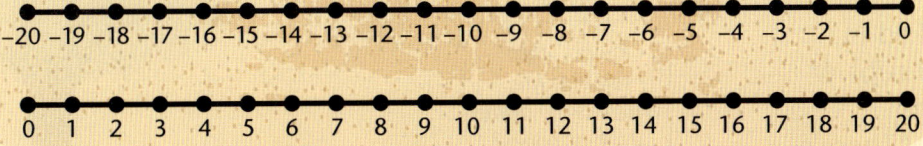

Use a number line to help with negative numbers. The number line can start and finish on any number.

Did you know?
At NASA, they use negative numbers to count to lift-off for space shuttle launches. They count the time before lift-off as negative numbers and the time after lift-off as positive numbers.
"Lift-off… –12 minutes." This means there are 12 minutes before lift-off.

Factor Tree Factory

Sir Ralph was scribbling numbers on his whiteboard.

"What are you doing?" asked Isabella.

"I'm in the middle of a **factor** tree investigation, to see if there are any patterns in the 'roots' numbers." Isabella was interested – trees with numbers for roots! She looked at the whiteboard.

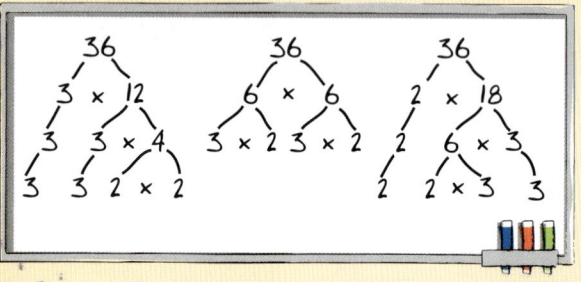

36 had been split into **multiples** in 3 different ways, but the 'root' numbers at the bottom were always two 3s and two 2s. Isabella wrote factor trees for 30. She had to think about the multiples of 30: all those numbers that could be divided exactly into 30.

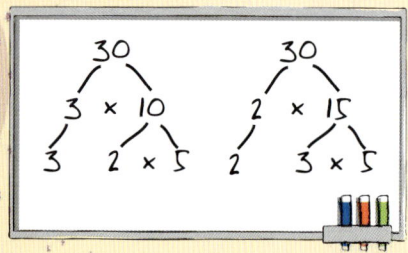

Just like Sir Ralph's diagram, the 'roots' had the same numbers although the multiplication facts were different. Isabella noticed that all the root numbers were **prime numbers**; they could not be divided any more. Isabella decided to multiply all the root numbers.

$3 \times 3 \times 2 \times 2 = 36$

$3 \times 2 \times 5 = 30$

Max walked in with two cups of tea for the workers. "There's a lot of work going on in here. It's like a little factory."

"A Factor Tree Factory!" laughed Isabella.

Max looked confused.

Roots... that reminds me. Where is my prime stash of bones?

Multiple machine

Sort the numbers 20–40 into the correct section of this Venn diagram.

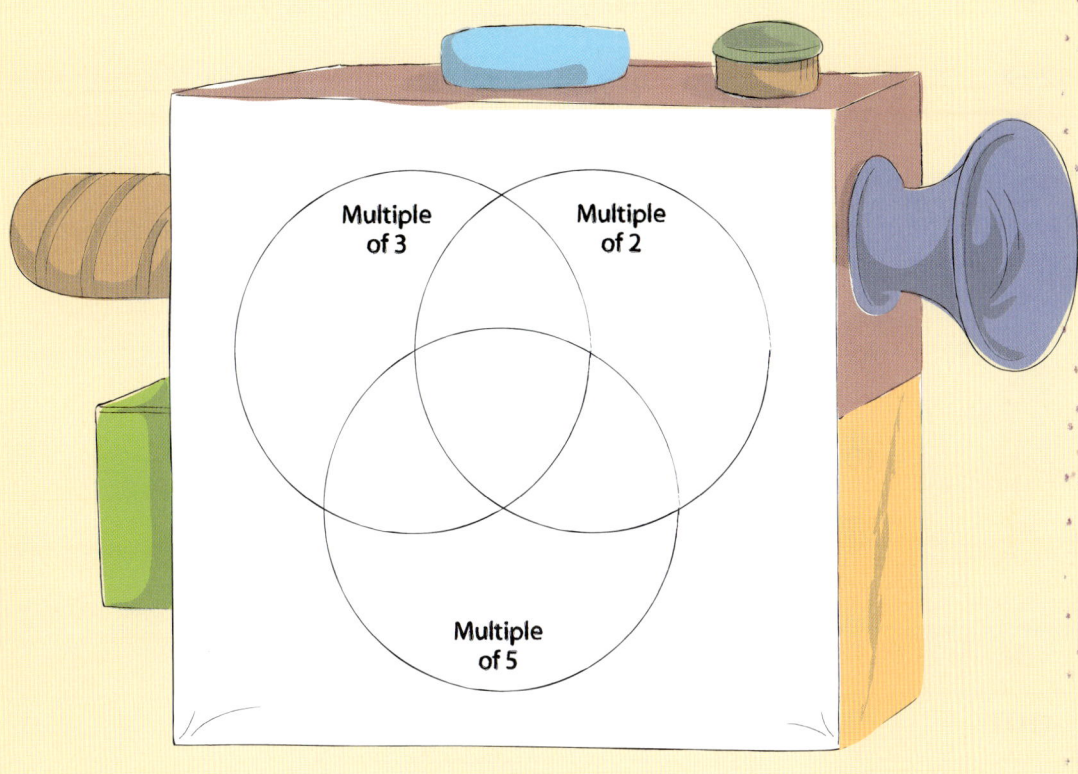

To check you have all the factors of a number, write them in pairs starting at 1 and going through each number in turn until you come to a number you have already used.
24   (1, 24)   (2, 12)   (3, 8)   (4, 6)
The next number would be 6,
which you've already used.

Did you know?
A **prime factor** is a factor that is a prime number. For example the factors of 12 are 1, 2, 3, 4, 6 and 12. The prime factors are 2 and 3.

Revise Time

1 Multiply each number by 100.

a 3 → _____   c 8.5 → _____   e 8.9 → _____

b 42 → _____   d 18.6 → _____   f 2.75 → _____

2 Look at the function machine, then write the missing numbers in this table.

IN	17		39		162	
OUT		45		14.5		29.9

3 Write these temperatures in order, starting with the lowest.

 3°C

1°C

−5°C

 −1°C

 0°C

8°C

−4°C

_____ _____ _____ _____ _____ _____ _____

4 What is the difference between these pairs of temperatures?

a −1°C   2°C   _____

b −4°C   −2°C _____

c 6°C   −5°C _____

d 0°C   −3°C _____

e −6°C   4°C   _____

5 Complete the factor pairs for these numbers.

a 18 (1, ___) (2, ___) (3, ___)

b 32 (1, ___) (2, ___) (4, ___)

c 40 (1, ___) (2, ___) (4, ___) (5, ___)

d 25 (1, ___) (5, ___)

e 36 (1, ___) (2, ___) (3, ___) (4, ___) (6, ___)

6 Write these numbers in the correct part of this Carroll diagram.

18   48   30   26   45   90   84   36   52   80

	Multiple of 3	Not a multiple of 3
Multiple of 4		
Not a multiple of 4		

Footy Fractions

Isabella was in her football kit, ready for her first match. Max was slicing the oranges. "Most football teams give slices of orange at half-time. It's a tradition," Max explained.

Max kept cutting up oranges into quarters until he had 13 quarters, one for each of the 11 players and the 2 substitutes. There were 3 slices left over.

"Oh no," said Max. "I forgot to count how many oranges I used, so I know for next week."

Isabella helped by counting the 13 quarters in the box. "That is $\frac{13}{4}$. One whole orange is 4 quarters or $\frac{4}{4}$."

She divided the 13 by 4, which was 3 whole oranges and 1 spare quarter.

On the table were 3 spare quarters, so Max had cut four oranges into quarters.

"That's good," said Max. "I'll cut 4 oranges each week and that will give 13 quarters for the team and 3 slices left over for us, which we can start eating now."

My kit's supposed to be orange in colour, not orange-shaped!

They slurped noisily on the orange slices. Max looked at Isabella and saw that the orange juice had dripped onto her T-shirt.

"It's a good job your kit is orange and not white," he laughed.

Whole goals

Colour in the balls showing fractions that make whole numbers and cross out the ones that make mixed numbers.

Top Tips!
It is easy to spot a fraction that is greater than one; the top number is greater than the bottom number.

Did you know?
Fractions greater than 1 are called **improper fractions**, e.g. $\frac{6}{5}$.
Mixed numbers are a mixture of whole numbers and fractions, e.g. $1\frac{1}{5}$.

Fair Testing

Isabella was setting up an experiment. She wanted to find out which things help plants to grow. She had a pack of 40 mixed seeds. $\frac{2}{5}$ of the seeds were poppies and $\frac{3}{5}$ were sunflowers.

To make a 'fair test' Isabella knew she had to use the same type of seed for all the tests. She decided to use the sunflower seeds and wanted to work out how many there were in the pack. Firstly, she worked out $\frac{1}{5}$ of 40 by dividing 40 by 5, which was 8. To work out $\frac{3}{5}$ of 40 she multiplied 8 by 3, which was 24. Isabella had calculated that there were 24 sunflower seeds in the pack.

In a 'fair test' Isabella knew she had to have one pot of seeds that were allowed to grow in a normal way, as a 'control'. She decided to use $\frac{1}{4}$ as the control and $\frac{3}{4}$ for the tests. To find $\frac{1}{4}$ of 24 Isabella divided 24 by 4, which gave 6 seeds. She placed them in a pot, watered them and placed the pot on the windowsill in the light. She had $\frac{3}{4}$ of the seeds left to experiment with. $\frac{3}{4}$ was the same as 3 lots of $\frac{1}{4}$. $3 \times 6 = 18$, so there were 18 seeds for the test.

I wonder if I'll grow taller if I stand in a dark cupboard?

Isabella wanted to put half in the light but with no water and half with water but in a cupboard with no light. She divided them into two groups of 9 seeds and put them in the light and dark.

Two weeks later Isabella put all the seeds together. The results were easy to see. The control group looked the healthiest, it had grown well and was a bright green. The seeds with light but no water had not grown at all. The seeds with water in the dark cupboard were very tall but a pale yellow colour.

Follow the fraction flowers

Find the trail through the flowers by following the correct answers.

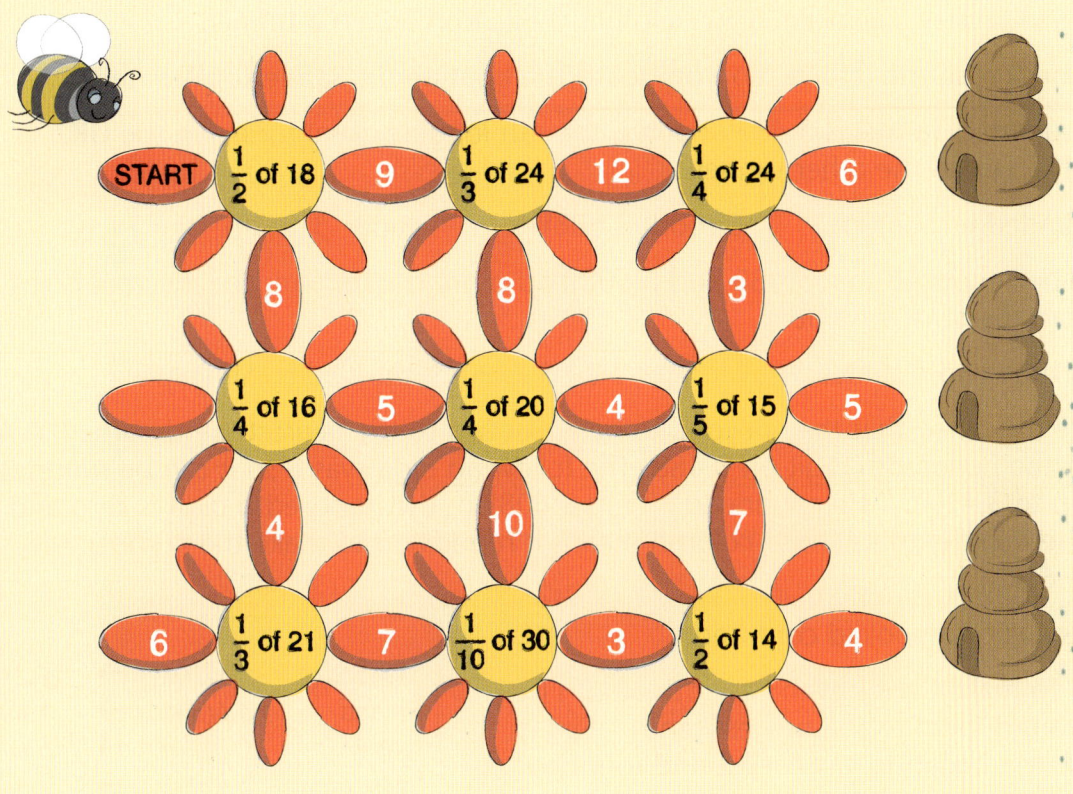

3/4 ← this is the **numerator**, it shows how many parts out of the whole are taken or used.

← this is the **denominator**, it shows how many parts the shape or number is divided into.

Did you know?
Percentages are fractions out of 100.
$\frac{3}{4}$ is the same as $\frac{75}{100}$ which is 75%.

Tunnel Travel

Sir Ralph, Max, Isabella and Spotless were having a trip on a canal boat.

"The canals were built to either go up hills by locks or just straight through the hills in tunnels," explained Sir Ralph as they approached a tunnel.

Isabella read the information on board the boat about Sapperton Tunnel.

'Sapperton Tunnel is 3.488km long, the 4th longest canal tunnel in the UK.' It then listed the other tunnels:

Standedge 5.21km   Strood 3.608km   Lapal 3.57km

Isabella noticed that 3.488 and 3.608 had more **digits** after the decimal point than the other numbers.

"These two distances look longer than 5.21km," she said to Sir Ralph.

He explained that they needed to be **rounded** to the nearest hundredth. "Look at the hundredth digit on 3.488. The following digit was 8 so it can be rounded up to 3.49km." He continued, "With 3.608km, the hundredth digit is zero and the 8 in the thousandth column means it rounds up to make the number 3.61km."

Isabella still looked confused.

"To make things even easier to read, I'll round them to the nearest tenth." Sir Ralph began to write a list and rounded the distances to the nearest tenth.

Standedge	5.21km	→ 5.2km
Strood	3.608km	→ 3.6km
Lapal	3.57km	→ 3.6km
Sapperton	3.488km	→ 3.5km

Sir Ralph had just finished when Max shouted to them, "Don't worry about rounding down. Worry about keeping your heads down! We're going into the tunnel!"

"What did you say?"

Round tunnels

Look at each tunnel and round the decimals to the nearest tenth or the nearest hundredth.

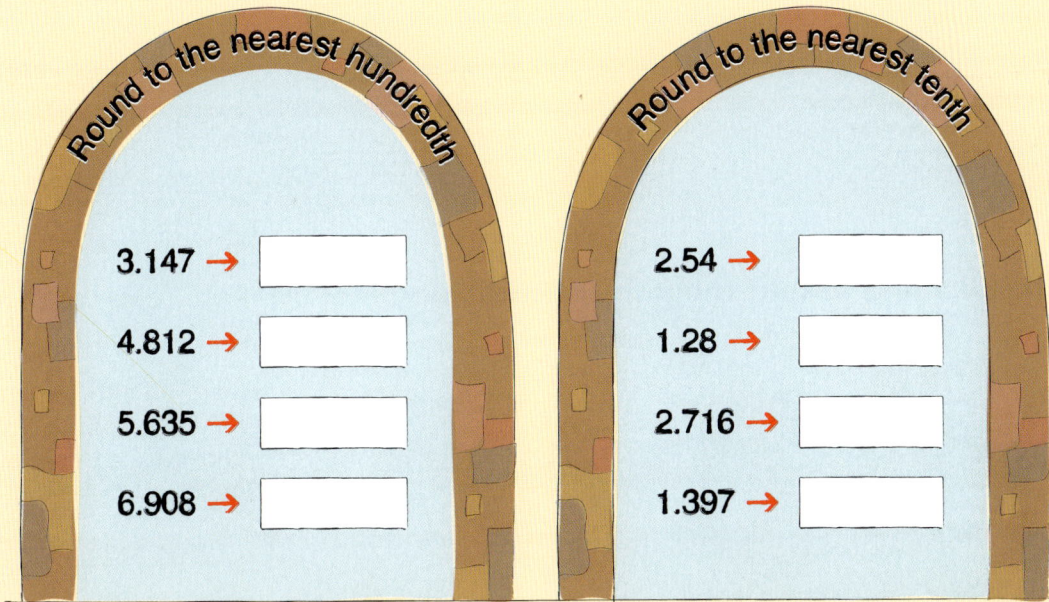

Round to the nearest hundredth
- 3.147 →
- 4.812 →
- 5.635 →
- 6.908 →

Round to the nearest tenth
- 2.54 →
- 1.28 →
- 2.716 →
- 1.397 →

Top Tips

Line numbers up, using headings to help.
These numbers are 463.612 and 8.97

hundreds	tens	units	tenths	hundredths	thousandths
		8 .	9	7	
4	6	3 .	6	1	2

Did you know?

3.4 is the same as $\frac{34}{10}$

5.26 is the same as $\frac{526}{100}$

Revise Time

1 Write these as mixed numbers.

a $\frac{14}{3}$ = ______

b $\frac{17}{5}$ = ______

c $\frac{11}{2}$ = ______

d $\frac{23}{5}$ = ______

e $\frac{21}{6}$ = ______

f $\frac{19}{4}$ = ______

2 Draw a line to join the pairs of matching fractions.

$8\frac{3}{4}$ $\frac{23}{4}$ $\frac{25}{3}$ $\frac{35}{4}$ $\frac{29}{3}$ $7\frac{1}{4}$ $\frac{26}{3}$

$8\frac{1}{3}$ $5\frac{3}{4}$ $9\frac{2}{3}$ $\frac{29}{4}$ $8\frac{2}{3}$

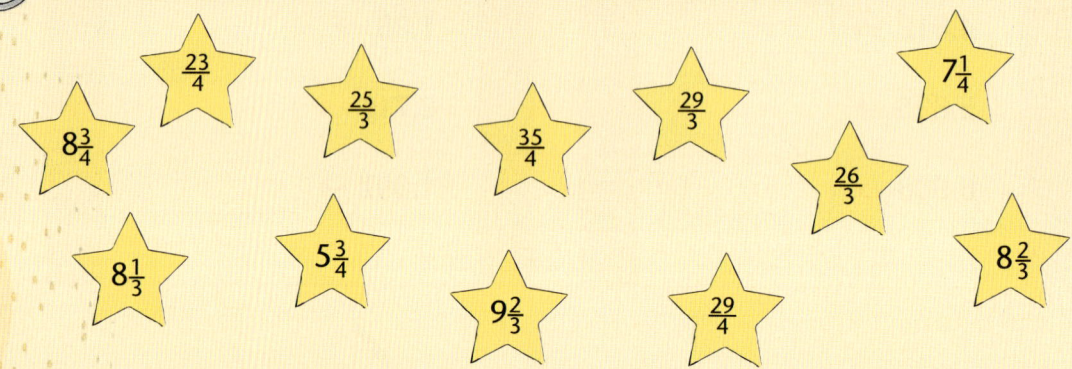

3 Draw a loop around $\frac{3}{4}$ of each set of seeds.

a

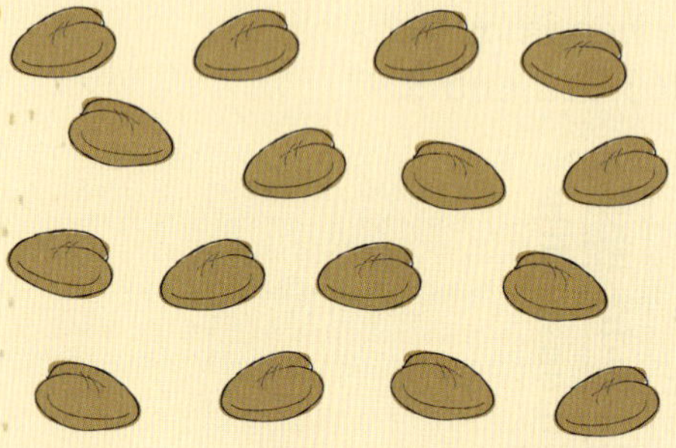

c

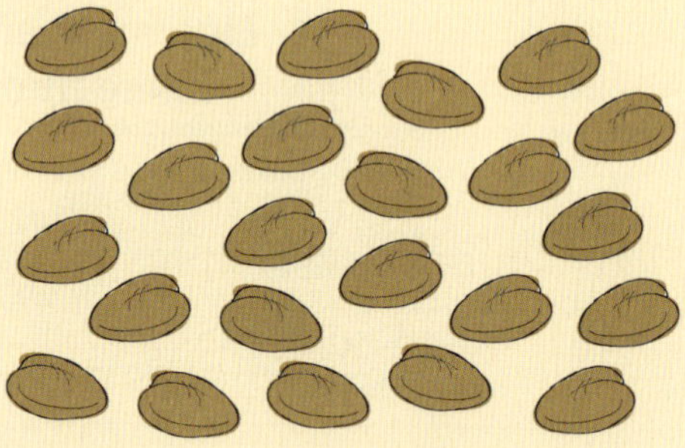

b

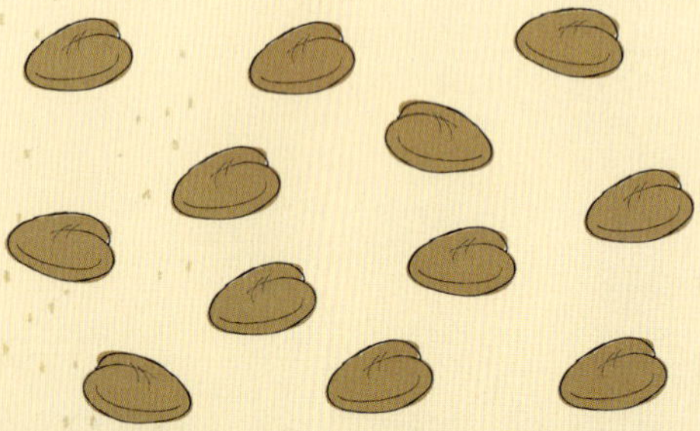

d

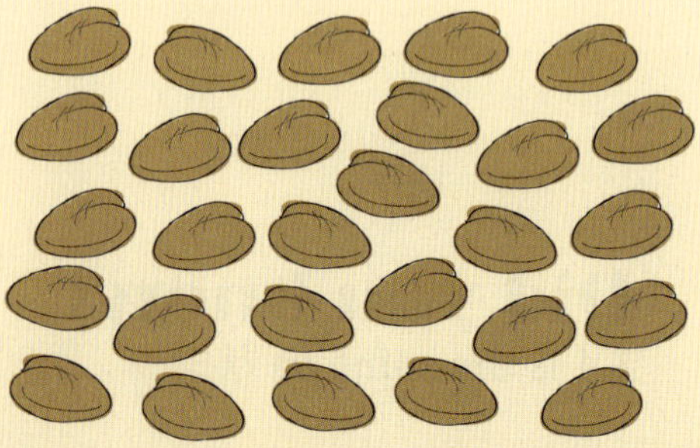

4 Answer these.

a $\frac{1}{4}$ of 48 = _____

b $\frac{1}{5}$ of 60 = _____

c $\frac{1}{6}$ of 42 = _____

d $\frac{1}{3}$ of 90 = _____

e $\frac{3}{4}$ of 36 = _____

f $\frac{1}{5}$ of 80 = _____

5 Write these decimals in order, starting with the smallest number.

3.58   3.08   3.805

3.85   3.8   3.588

_____ _____ _____ _____ _____ _____

6 Round these decimals to the nearest tenth.

a 12.55 _____

b 0.19 _____

c 6.84 _____

d 8.44 _____

e 1.748 _____

f 9.083 _____

Chicken Run

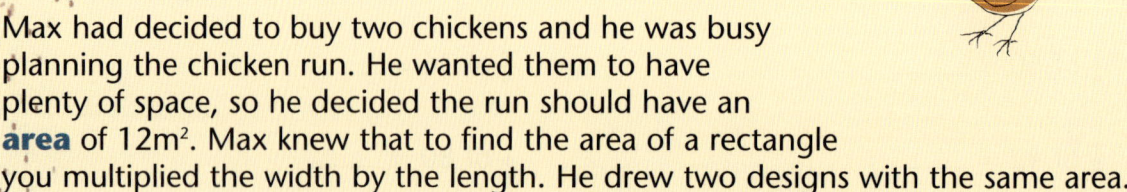

Max had decided to buy two chickens and he was busy planning the chicken run. He wanted them to have plenty of space, so he decided the run should have an **area** of 12m². Max knew that to find the area of a rectangle you multiplied the width by the length. He drew two designs with the same area.

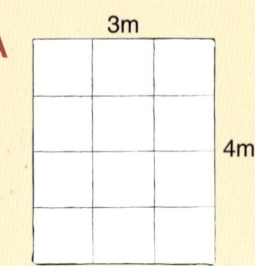

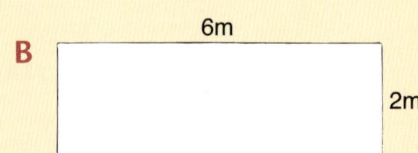

Design A   3m × 4m = 12m²   Design B   2m × 6m = 12m²

Max needed to work out the **perimeter** of each chicken run to know the length of the chicken wire he needed. He added together all the sides for each design and found out that they had the same area but not the same perimeter.

Design A Perimeter   3m + 4m + 3m + 4m = 14m

Design B Perimeter   2m + 2m + 6m + 6m = 16m

Max decided he wanted something a bit more exciting, so he designed some more interestingly shaped chicken runs.

To work out the areas of these odd shapes, Max imagined them as two rectangles, and worked out the area of each part and added them together.

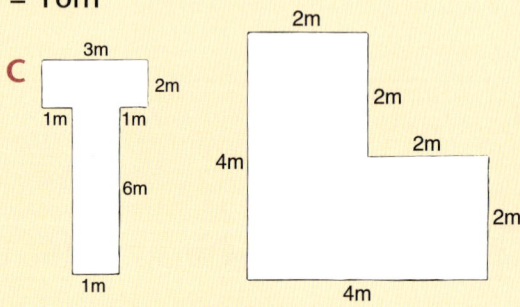

Area of Design C
2m × 3m = 6m²   6m × 1m = 6m²   6m² + 6m² = 12m²

Area of Design D
2m × 2m = 4m²   4m × 2m = 8m²   4m² + 8m² = 12m²

To find the perimeter of these shapes, Max added together all the sides. Design C had a perimeter of 22m and Design D had a perimeter of 16m.

Max decided Design C was best, as it would give the chickens the longest distance to walk round the perimeter.

Your chickens are on the run, not in the run!

Chicken pen plans

Calculate the area and perimeter of each of these plans.

a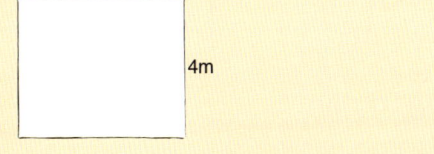

area = _____ m²   perimeter = _____ m

c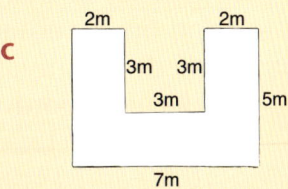

area = _____ m²   perimeter = _____ m

b

area = _____ m²   perimeter = _____ m

d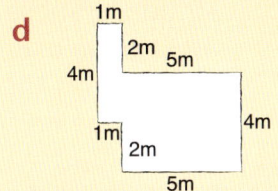

area = _____ m²   perimeter = _____ m

e   Which shape has the largest perimeter?   _____

f   Which shape has the largest area?   _____

Top Tips!

You can use formulae to show the area and perimeter of rectangles.
Area = L × W
Perimeter = 2 × (L + W)
L stands for length and W stands for width.

Did you know?

Area is written as cm² or centimetre squared. That is exactly what it means; you are counting how many 1cm × 1cm squares there are in a shape. Drawing centimetre markers on each side or even drawing the squares may help you. But it takes longer, and it is easier to multiply the two sides.

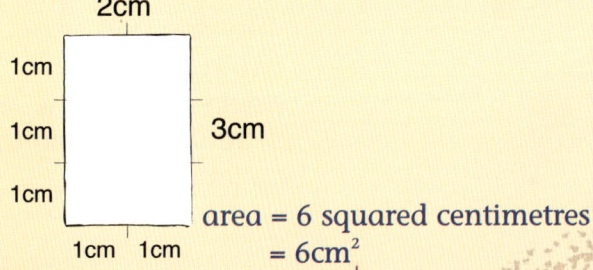

area = 6 squared centimetres = 6cm²

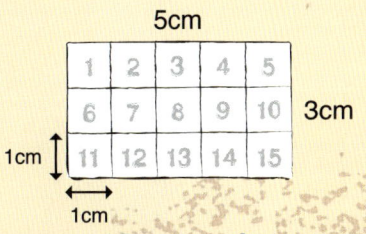

area = 15 squared centimetres = 15cm²

Train Times

Isabella and Sir Ralph were going to London for the day. Isabella was checking times of trains from Oxford to London on a website. The first page asked what time they wanted to leave Oxford. It gave a selection of times 08:00, 09:00, 10:00 and 11:00 and some earlier and later times. Sir Ralph thought 10 o'clock would be the best; it would give them plenty of time to get to the station. Isabella selected 10:00 and pressed 'next'. The next page asked what time they wanted to leave London on their return journey. Sir Ralph said they would be finished in London at about 7 o'clock.

Isabella clicked on 07:00 and then pressed 'next'. Something was wrong; the next page said there was an error.

On the screen was written, "You cannot select a return train earlier than your train leaving Oxford."

Isabella and Sir Ralph looked at the information and realised they had clicked on 7 o'clock in the morning. Sir Ralph scrolled through the times until he came to 19:00.

"That's better, this is 7 o'clock in the evening," he told Isabella, as he selected 19:00.

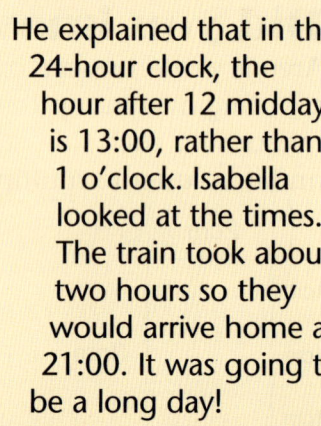

Departure times:

07:00
08:00
09:00
10:00
11:00
12:00
13:00
14:00
15:00
16:00
17:00
18:00
19:00
20:00
21:00
22:00

21:00? It's way past Izzy's bedtime!

He explained that in the 24-hour clock, the hour after 12 midday is 13:00, rather than 1 o'clock. Isabella looked at the times. The train took about two hours so they would arrive home at 21:00. It was going to be a long day!

Triple time

Draw lines to join the matching times.

5 past 4 in the afternoon	3.00pm	0745
quarter to 8 in the morning	10.30pm	1315
half past 10 at night	9.50am	1500
10 to 10 in the morning	7.45am	1605
quarter past 1 in the afternoon	4.05pm	0950
3 o'clock in the afternoon	1.15pm	2230

Top Tips

When using 12-hour time, use am for morning and pm for evening.
So 8 o'clock in the morning is 8.00am or 08:00, and 8 o'clock in the evening is 8.00pm or 20:00.

Did you know?
These times have only one minute between them:

23:59 → 00:00 → 00:01
one minute before midnight → midnight → one minute past midnight

11:59 → 12:00 → 12:01
one minute before midday → midday → one minute after midday

Spreading Jam

Max had been selling his speciality jams to local shops for over a year. He only had a few jars left and needed to make some more. The strawberry and raspberry jams had sold very well throughout the whole year, but he needed to check the other two flavours. He plotted the number of sales onto a graph. This would make it easier to compare the number of jars sold.

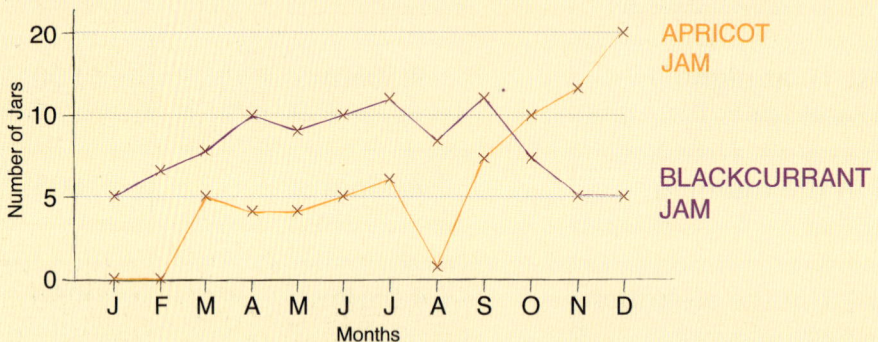

He looked at the purple line for blackcurrant jam first. He looked at the overall shape of the line and could see a slight rise in the middle. Then he looked at the lowest and highest points. The most sold in one month was 12 jars in July and September and the least was 5 jars in three different months. He decided that he would make smaller amounts in the winter and more between April and September.

Now to check the sales of apricot jam. This line was quite different, staying quite low all year until it rose in September. In December he sold 20 jars, but no jars had been sold in January and February.

Max thought about this. "Oh I get it," he said to himself, "Christmas cakes! Apricot jam is used in Christmas cakes! People must start to think about what they need for Christmas from about September."

Max felt pleased with his powers of deduction, and decided that he would only make apricot jam between September and December.

Well, this really is a traffic jam!

Paddling pool sales

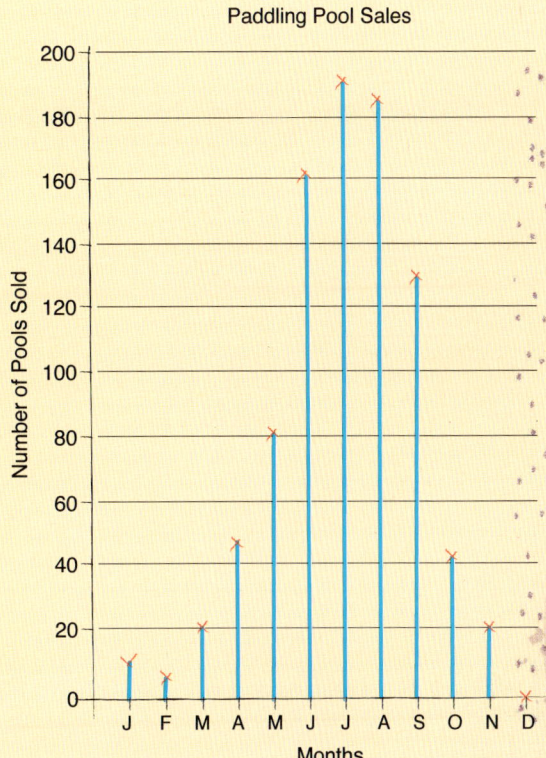

Paddling Pool Sales

a In which month were the most paddling pools sold?

_____

b In which month were no pools sold?

_____

c In which two months were the same number sold?

_____

d Why do you think more pools were sold in June, July and August?

_____

_____

Read the labels carefully to know exactly what information the graph is giving.
Graphs can be drawn with a different range of numbers and, although the information is the same, it can look different.

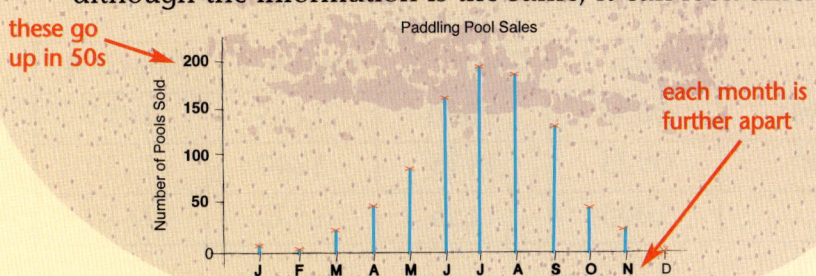

Did you know?

A conversion graph is a straight-line graph. It shows one value converted to another.

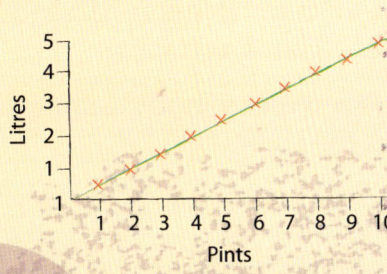

33

Revise Time

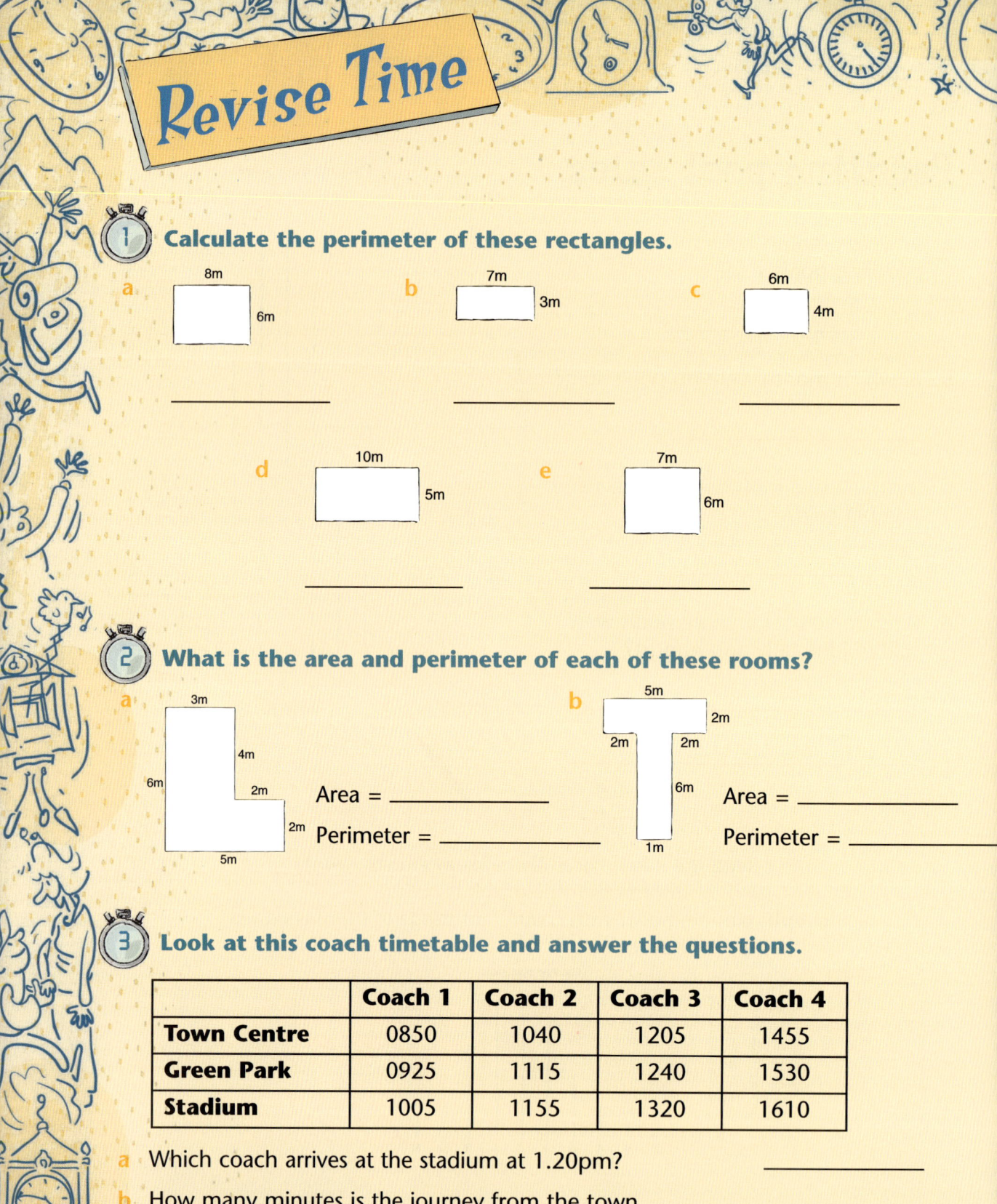

1 Calculate the perimeter of these rectangles.

a) 8m × 6m _____

b) 7m × 3m _____

c) 6m × 4m _____

d) 10m × 5m _____

e) 7m × 6m _____

2 What is the area and perimeter of each of these rooms?

a) (L-shape: 3m, 4m, 2m, 2m, 5m, 6m)
Area = _____
Perimeter = _____

b) (T-shape: 5m, 2m, 2m, 2m, 6m, 1m)
Area = _____
Perimeter = _____

3 Look at this coach timetable and answer the questions.

	Coach 1	Coach 2	Coach 3	Coach 4
Town Centre	0850	1040	1205	1455
Green Park	0925	1115	1240	1530
Stadium	1005	1155	1320	1610

a) Which coach arrives at the stadium at 1.20pm? _____

b) How many minutes is the journey from the town centre to Green Park? _____

c) How many minutes is the journey from Green Park to the stadium? _____

d) Which coach leaves the town centre just before 3.00pm? _____

4 Write the matching times. The first one is done for you.

2.50pm	14:50
	21:35
6.40am	
	10:55
10.05pm	
	17:25

5 This graph shows the number of televisions sold in six months.

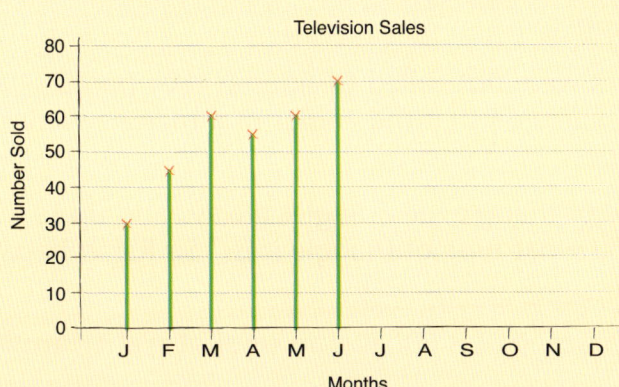

a In which month were 70 televisions sold? _____

b How many televisions were sold in April? _____

c How many more televisions were sold in June than in March? _____

d How many televisions were sold altogether in January and February? _____

6 Capacity can be measured in litres and pints.
This graph converts litres to pints.

2 litres is approximately 3.5 pints.

a How many pints are approximately the same as:

4 litres → _____   3 litres → _____

5 litres → _____

b How many litres are approximately the same as:

9 pints → _____   6 pints → _____

2 pints → _____

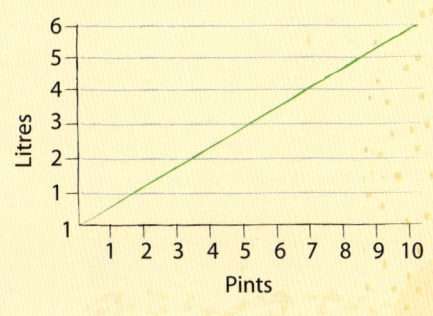

Tricky Triangles

Isabella was helping Sir Ralph in his laboratory.

"Pass me the tripod, please," he asked Isabella.

"Why is it called a tripod?" she replied, handing it over.

Sir Ralph explained that 'tri' means 3 and the stand has 3 sides, 3 corners and 3 legs. "Another word for leg is 'pod' so tripod means 3-legs."

"Other words are similar," continued Sir Ralph, "such as triangle, meaning 3 angles, triplets, meaning 3 babies born together and my favourite – triceratops – a 3-horned dinosaur!"

Isabella wondered why triangles were not called tri-sides as they had 3 sides as well as 3 angles. Sir Ralph explained that the angles of a triangle were far more interesting than their sides.

"No matter what size or type of triangle, all 3 angles always add up to 180°. Also, the angles tell you what type of triangle it is." Sir Ralph began drawing on the whiteboard.

"If all the angles are equal in size, that is 60°, it is an **equilateral triangle**."

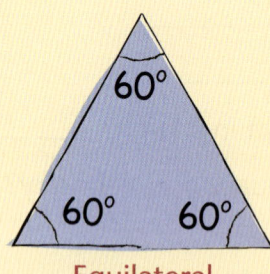
Equilateral

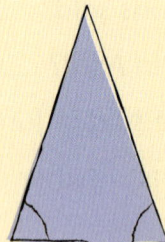
Isosceles

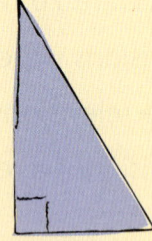
Right-angled

Scalene

The triceraspot ruled the earth for thousands of years...

"If two of the angles are the same size it is an **isosceles triangle**.

"A triangle with a right angle is a **right-angled triangle**.

"A **scalene triangle** has no angles or sides the same and no right angle."

Isabella wasn't keen on the scalene triangle. "It sounds all scaly and slimy – no wonder it's nothing special!"

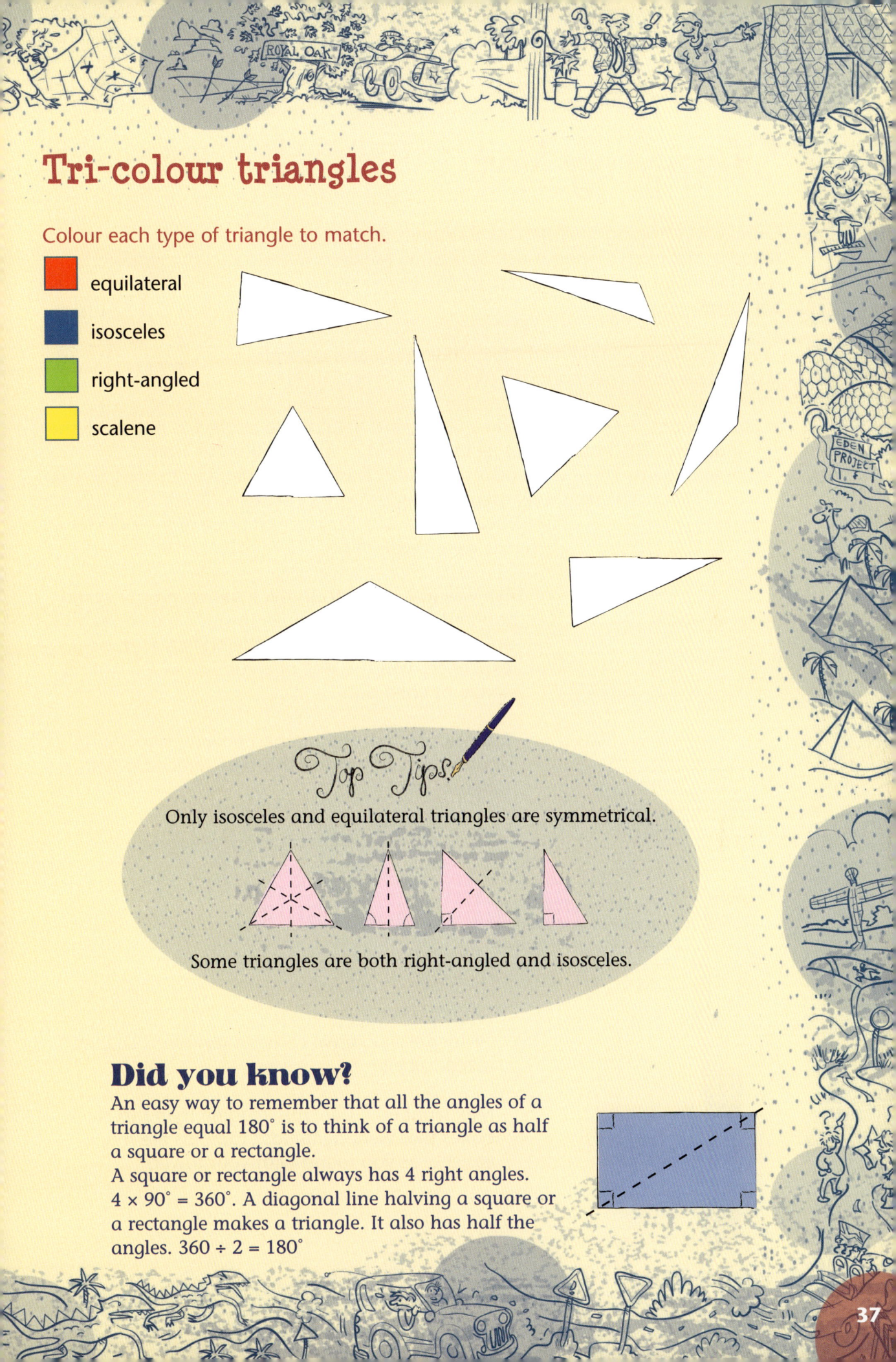

Tri-colour triangles

Colour each type of triangle to match.

- 🟥 equilateral
- 🟦 isosceles
- 🟩 right-angled
- 🟨 scalene

Top Tips

Only isosceles and equilateral triangles are symmetrical.

Some triangles are both right-angled and isosceles.

Did you know?

An easy way to remember that all the angles of a triangle equal 180° is to think of a triangle as half a square or a rectangle.
A square or rectangle always has 4 right angles.
4 × 90° = 360°. A diagonal line halving a square or a rectangle makes a triangle. It also has half the angles. 360 ÷ 2 = 180°

Shopping Net

Isabella was helping Max unpack the shopping. Actually, she wasn't being much help at all as she was having great fun trying to stack the boxes into a tall tower.

"Yes, very clever," exclaimed Max, "but you'll end up with crushed cereal in that bottom box."

She thought she had better be a little more helpful and started to put away the shopping. She noticed that all the **cuboid** shapes were made from cardboard. There were boxes of cereal, washing powder and cartons of fruit juice. The next most popular shapes were **cylinders**. There were cans of baked beans, soup and fizzy drinks. Most of the cylinder shapes were made of tin.

Max was just going to throw away an empty cereal box, but instead he carefully unstuck the edges and unfolded the box until it was lying flat. This, he explained, was the **net** of a cuboid, which was its shape opened out.

Isabella saw that the net had 6 faces. Max took another cereal box and this time opened it in a different way.

It would be difficult if this was cube shaped; the paper wouldn't roll off very easily!

"Why doesn't cereal come in **pyramid** shapes?" asked Isabella.

Max laughed, "Can you imagine trying to stack boxes that were pyramids? Cuboids are much easier… as you found with your tower!"

Cube challenge

There are many different nets for a cube. Draw four more nets on this grid.

Top Tips

To work out the shape of a net, count the **faces** and look at the shape of the faces. All cuboids and cubes have six rectangular faces, a cube has 6 square faces.

Did you know?

Nets of pyramids always have at least 4 triangular faces.

Car Treasure Hunt

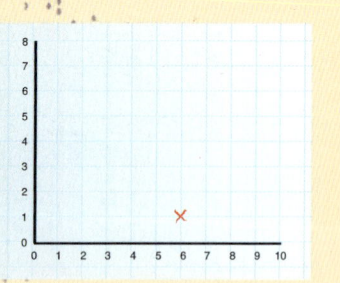

It was the day of the village fête, and the highlight of the day was the village treasure hunt. The Witherbottoms loved treasure hunts, and were keen to win it again, as they normally did! This one was a little different though. The clues led to 8 different places, where pairs of numbers were written down on small boards. These were **coordinates** that needed plotting as points on a grid given at the start of the treasure hunt. Once all the coordinates were found, the points could be joined to make a secret shape.

The first clue was tricky:

> We're looking for a road so keep calm,
> Your clue could be a loud alarm

They all thought long and hard. Suddenly, Sir Ralph shouted, "I've got it! Bell Lane!"

They drove off and, sure enough, there was the first pair of coordinates: (6, 1).

Sir Ralph showed Isabella how to plot the point. "The first number is the one across the bottom so follow it along to 6 with your finger. The next number is 1, so you go up 1 square. Draw a cross to show (6, 1)."

Isabella plotted this point and they then looked at the next clue.

> The first part of this is blue blood,
> the second part hid Robin Hood

Isabella looked very confused, but Max worked it out and explained it to her. "Well, blue blood is royal blood and Robin Hood hid in an oak tree, so it's the Royal Oak!"

They drove to the Royal Oak and on the door were the coordinates (7, 4). They drew a cross at this point and then joined the two points.

They now knew what they were doing and sped around the countryside finding the coordinates for the 8 points:

(6, 1) (7, 4) (9, 5) (7, 6) (6, 8) (5, 6) (3, 5) (5, 4)

They looked at the completed grid.

> If motor racing included reading coordinates, I'd be the world champion!

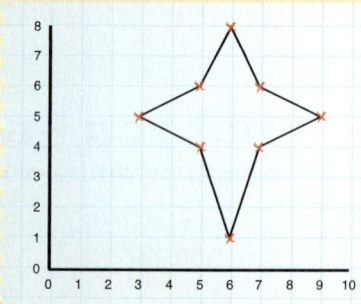

"We're real stars," said Sir Ralph. "Shall we go to the Royal Oak to celebrate?"

Growing shapes

a Join these 15 coordinates in order on the grid.

(0, 3) → (1, 3) → (2, 4) → (2, 3) →
(5, 3) → (6, 4) → (6, 0) → (5, 0) →
(5, 1) → (3, 1) → (3, 0) → (2, 0) →
(2, 2) → (0, 2) → (0, 3)

Plot these points then draw the new pictures. Try –

b doubling the first coordinate

c doubling the second coordinate

d doubling both coordinates

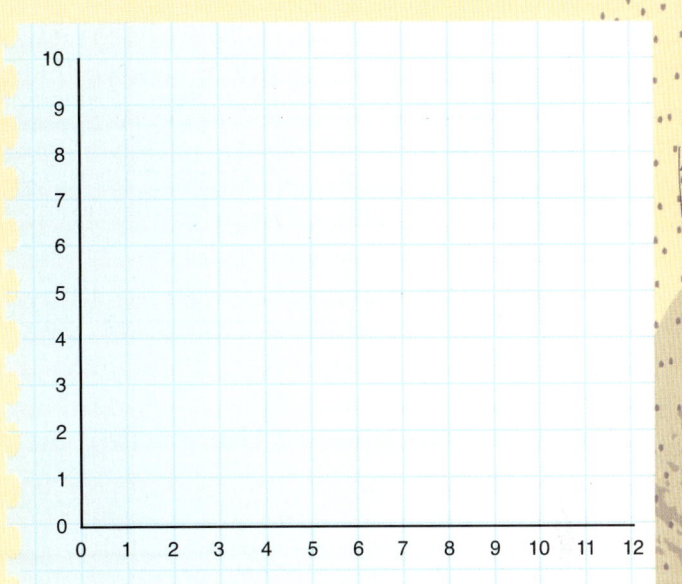

Top Tips

The numbers on the horizontal x-axis are written first, then the y-axis. You can remember to plot x before y because x comes before y in the alphabet.

Did you know?

Coordinates can also use negative numbers to show a position. This cross is at (−3, 2)

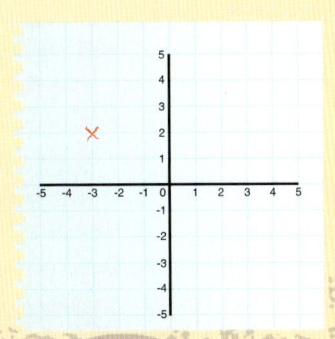

Revise Time

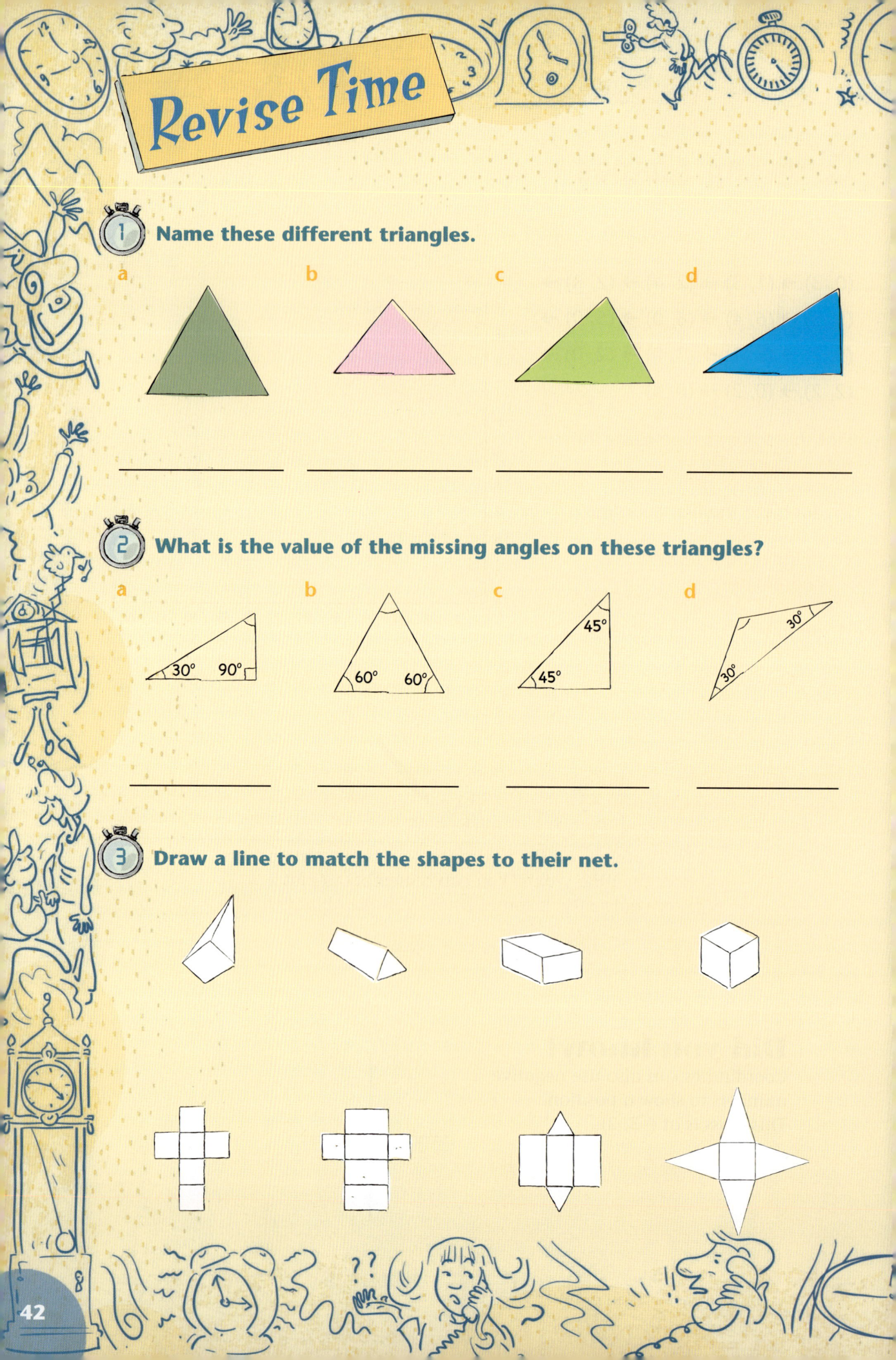

1 Name these different triangles.

a   b   c   d

_____

2 What is the value of the missing angles on these triangles?

a   b   c   d

a) 30°, 90°   b) 60°, 60°   c) 45°, 45°   d) 30°, 30°

_____

3 Draw a line to match the shapes to their net.

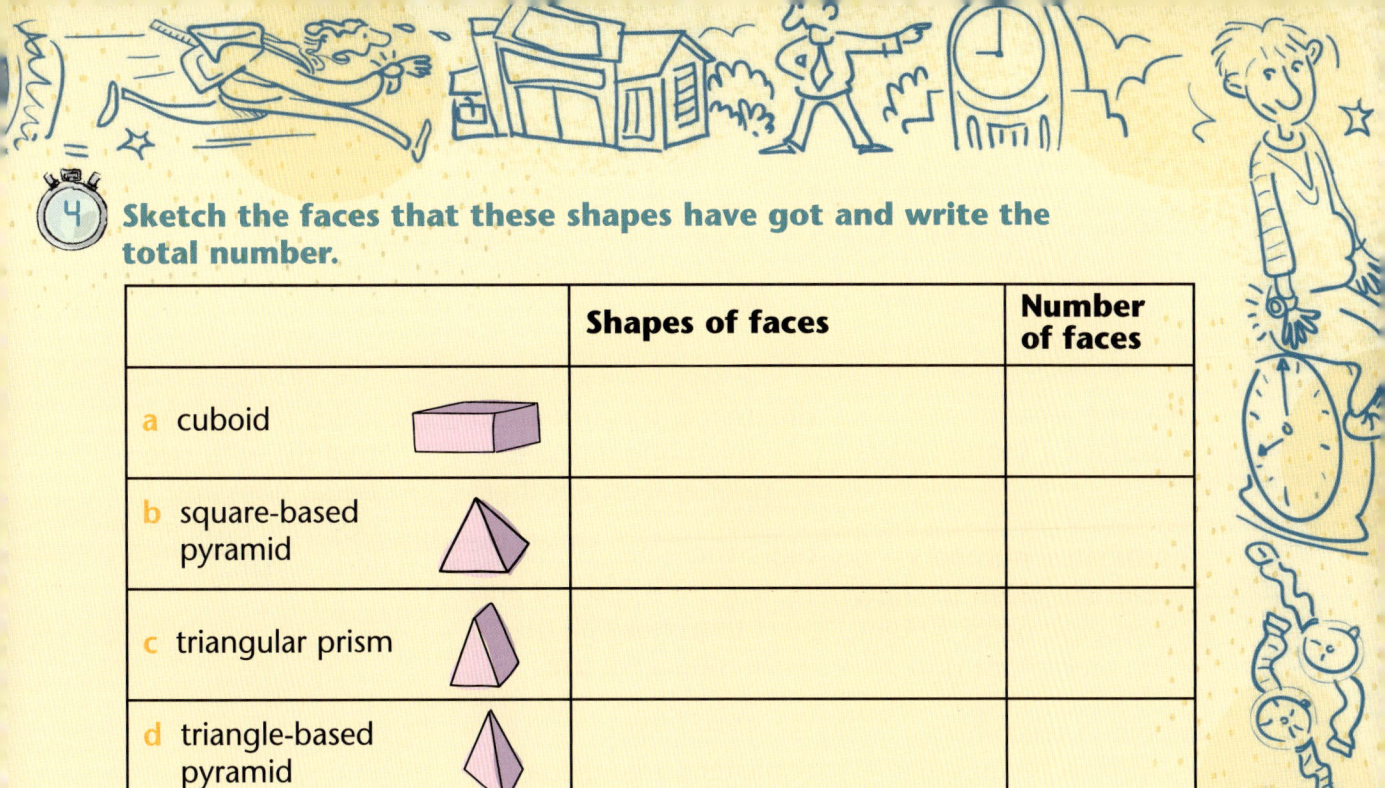

4 Sketch the faces that these shapes have got and write the total number.

	Shapes of faces	Number of faces
a cuboid		
b square-based pyramid		
c triangular prism		
d triangle-based pyramid		

5 Plot these points on this grid.

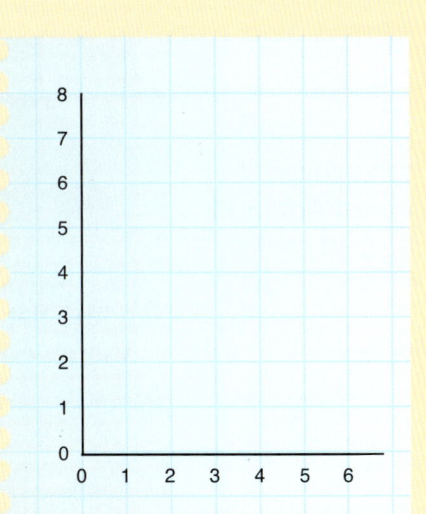

a (3, 5)
b (4, 4)
c (0, 3)
d (2, 7)
e (5, 8)

6 Write the coordinates for each of the crosses on this grid.

a _____
b _____
c _____
d _____
e _____

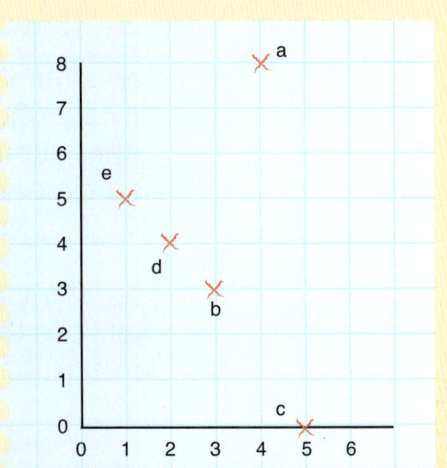

Glossary

area the amount of surface a shape covers

coordinates numbers that are given to show the position of a point on a graph or grid

cuboid a solid shape with six rectangular faces. Two of the faces could be square

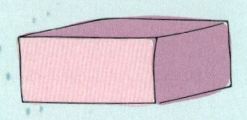

cylinder a solid shape with a curved side and the same sized circles at either end

denominator the bottom number of a fraction, the number of parts it is divided into, e.g. $\frac{2}{3}$

difference the amount by which one number is greater than another

digit there are 10 digits: 0 1 2 3 4 5 6 7 8 and 9 that make all the numbers we use

equilateral triangle a triangle with all sides and angles the same size

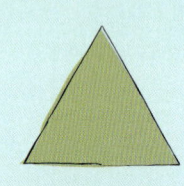

face the flat side of a 3D shape

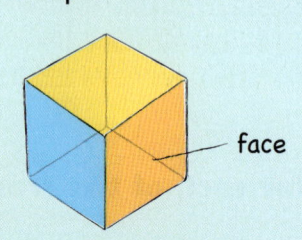

factor a number that will divide exactly into other numbers, e.g. 5 is a factor of 20

improper fractions fractions that are greater than 1, e.g. $\frac{5}{2}$

isosceles triangle a triangle with two equal sides and opposite base angles also equal

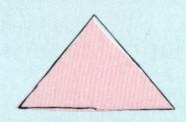

mixed numbers a mixture of whole numbers and fractions, e.g. $2\frac{1}{2}$

multiple a number made by multiplying together two other numbers

negative number a number that is less than zero

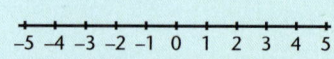

−5 −4 −3 −2 −1 0 1 2 3 4 5

net what a 3D shape looks like when it's opened out flat

numerator the top number of a fraction, e.g. $\frac{3}{5}$

palindrome a number or word that reads the same forwards and backwards

percentages (%) fractions out of 100, e.g. 30% means 30 out of 100

perimeter the distance all the way around the edge of a shape or object

prime factor a factor that is a prime number

prime numbers numbers that can only be divided exactly by either themselves or 1

pyramid a solid shape with triangular faces that meet at a point

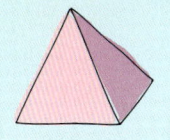

remainder if a number cannot be divided exactly by another number, it leaves a whole number answer and a remainder or an amount left over

right-angled triangle a triangle with one right angle

rounding rounding a number means changing it to the nearest ten, hundred or thousand, or changing a decimal to the nearest tenth, hundredth or whole number

scalene triangle a triangle with no equal sides or angles

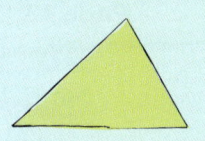

total the total is the result when you add together a group of numbers

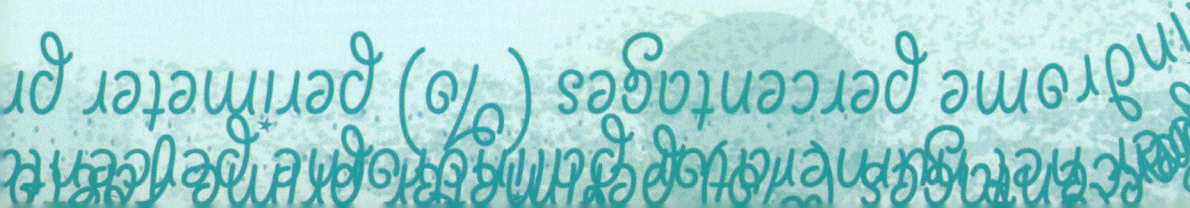

Answers

Page 5
a 202 → mum
b 4664 → peep
c 21512 → madam
d 31513 → radar

Page 7

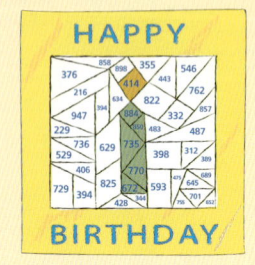

Page 9

Pages 10–11 Revision exercises

Exercise 1
a 2084
b 45
c 792, 1088
d 849, 1190

Exercise 2
a 5492
b 5891
c 7935
d 882
e 1079
f 919

Exercise 3
a 8
b 7
c 4
d 8
e 8, 4

Exercise 4

a

×	20	7
40	800	280
2	40	14

1080
54
1134

b

×	10	9
30	300	270
8	80	72

570
152
722

c

×	20	3
40	800	120
2	40	6

920
46
966

d

×	20	3
30	600	90
6	120	18

690
138
828

e

×	40	5
20	800	100
8	320	40

900
360
1260

Exercise 5
a r2
b r1
c r1
d r4
e r5
f r3

Exercise 6
a 425, 780
b 677, 425
c 762, 780
d 677, 116, 425

Page 13

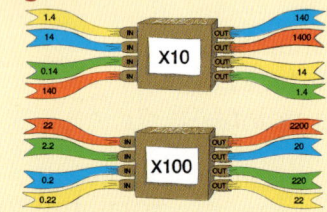

Page 15

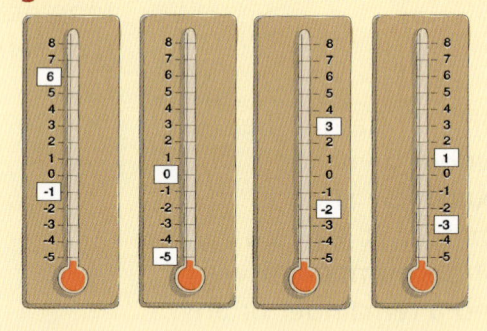

Page 17

Pages 18–19 Revision exercises
Exercise 1
a 300
b 4200
c 850
d 1860
e 890
f 275

Exercise 2

IN	17	450	39	145	162	299
OUT	1.7	45	3.9	14.5	16.2	29.9

Exercise 3
−5°C, −4°C, −1°C, 0°C, 1°C, 3°C, 8°C

Exercise 4
a 3
b 2
c 11
d 3
e 10

Exercise 5
a (1, 18) (2, 9) (3, 6)
b (1, 32) (2, 16) (4, 8)
c (1, 40) (2, 20) (4, 10) (5, 8)
d (1, 25) (5, 5)
e (1, 36) (2, 18) (3, 12) (4, 9) (6, 6)

Exercise 6

	Multiple of 3	Not a multiple of 3
Multiple of 4	48, 84, 36	52, 80
Not a multiple of 4	18, 30, 90, 45	26

Page 21

Page 23

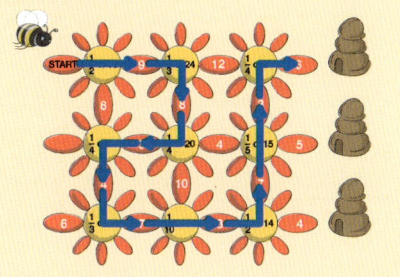

Page 25
3.147 → 3.15
4.812 → 4.81
5.635 → 5.64
6.908 → 6.91

2.54 → 2.5
1.28 → 1.3
2.716 → 2.7
1.397 → 1.4

Pages 26–27 Revision exercises
Exercise 1
a $4\frac{2}{3}$
b $3\frac{2}{5}$
c $5\frac{1}{2}$
d $4\frac{3}{5}$
e $3\frac{3}{6}$ or $3\frac{1}{2}$
f $4\frac{3}{4}$

Exercise 2

Exercise 3
a circle any 12 seeds
b circle any 9 seeds
c circle any 18 seeds
d circle any 21 seeds

Exercise 4
a 12
b 12
c 7
d 30
e 27
f 16

Exercise 5
3.08, 3.58, 3.588, 3.8, 3.805, 3.85

Exercise 6
a 12.6
b 0.2
c 6.8
d 8.4
e 1.7
f 9.1

Page 29
a area = 20m², perimeter = 18m
b area = 21m², perimeter = 20m
c area = 26m², perimeter = 30m
d area = 24m², perimeter = 24m
e shape c
f shape c

Page 31

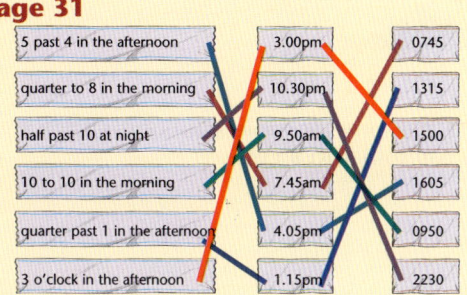

Page 33
a July
b December
c March and November
d Paddling pools are used in the summer.

Pages 34–35 Revision exercises
Exercise 1
a 28m   d 30m
b 20m   e 26m
c 20m

Exercise 2
a area = 22m², perimeter = 22m
b area = 16m², perimeter = 26m

Exercise 3
a Coach 3   c 40 minutes
b 35 minutes   d Coach 4

Exercise 4
2.50pm → 14:50
9.35am → 21:35
6.40am → 06:40
10.55am → 10:55
10.05pm → 22:05
5.25pm → 17:25

Exercise 5
a June   c 10
b 55   d 75

Exercise 6
a 4 litres → 7 pints
3 litres → 5.25 or $5\frac{1}{4}$ pints
5 litres → 8.75 or $8\frac{3}{4}$ pints
b 9 pints → 5 litres
6 pints → 3.5 or $3\frac{1}{2}$ litres
2 pints → 1 litre

Page 37

Page 39
These are some possible solutions. Check the nets can fold into a cube

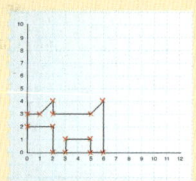

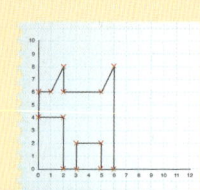

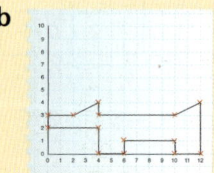

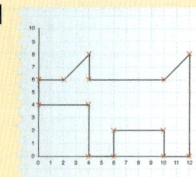

Page 41
a, b, c, d (graphs)

Pages 42–43 Revision exercises
Exercise 1
a equilateral   c scalene
b isosceles   d right-angled

Exercise 2
a 60°   c 90°
b 60°   d 120°

Exercise 3

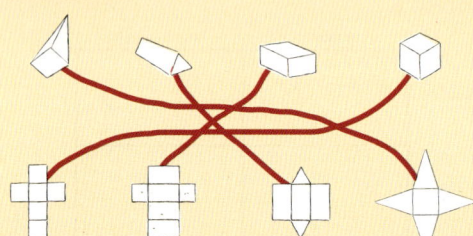

Exercise 4

	Shapes of faces	Number of faces
a cuboid		6
b square-based pyramid		5
c triangular prism		5
d triangle-based pyramid		4

Exercise 5

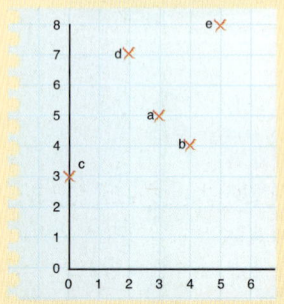

Exercise 6
a (4, 8)   d (2, 4)
b (3, 3)   e (1, 5)
c (5, 0)